PORTRAITS OF
HOPE

PORTRAITS OF
HOPE

PRESENTED BY

Respecting People. Impacting Business.™

International Headquarters
9701 Boardwalk Boulevard
Oklahoma City, OK 73162
ExpressPros.com

PUBLISHED BY

© Copyright 2014 by Express Services, Inc.

All rights reserved. This book or any portion thereof may not be reproduced
or used in any manner whatsoever without the prior written permission
of Express Services, Inc., except in the case of brief quotations
in noncommercial uses permitted by copyright law.
For permission requests, write to Express Services, Inc., addressed
"Attention: Marketing and Communications Vice President,"
at the address below.

Express Services, Inc.
9701 Boardwalk Boulevard
Oklahoma City, OK 73162

To learn more about Express Services, Inc. and Express Employment Professionals,
we invite you to visit us online at ExpressPros.com.

Printed in the United States by Southwestern Printing.

ISBN 978-0-615-94728-0

Designed by k lowe creative.

First Edition

Cover Photos Courtesy of:
Roger Wyan Photography
Jim Stafford Photography
David DuPuy Photography and Videography
Lindsay Wogen Photography
Daniel Sheehan Photography
Carol Hansen Photography, LLC.
Ed Clark Photography, Inc.

TABLE OF CONTENTS

Foreword i

Acknowledgments iii

Their Quotes iv

Their Stories 1

Janice Andrick 3

Meghan Andryski 4

Mary Bailey 6

Josh Baughman 9

Jim Britton 10

Wakina Buxton-Frazier 12

Randall and Pat Camp 15

Amy Clegg 17

Mary Ann Cummings 18

Greg and Rina Donaldson 20

Garrett Fairbanks 23

Rocky Gill 25

Chris Green 26

Jonathan Groeger 29

Pedro Guerrero 30

Mark and Sandy Hagen 33

Carrie Harmes 34

Ruben Herrera 36

Lindon Hibbert 39

TABLE OF CONTENTS

Debbie Joswick 41

Heather Koontz and Evan Brazille 42

Terry Lampe 44

Betsy Lindgren. 47

Roberta Long 48

Inder Narang 51

Debi Nimz 52

Tina Padilla 55

Joe Paquette 57

Megan Plopper 58

Sherry Preston. 61

Renee Rodriguez 62

Helen Simmons 65

Frank Robert Smith 66

Christy Taylor 69

Eric Urban 71

Deidra Viney 72

Lorenzo Thomas Wallace 74

Felicia Walls. 77

Murray Glenn Whitaker 78

Izeal Wilson. 80

Christopher Yaniz 83

Dawn Yengich 84

FOREWORD

As CEO, President, and Chairman of the Board of Express Employment Professionals, every day I see firsthand the difference a job can make—the hope and fulfillment it can bring to people's lives.

Like former U.S. President Ronald Reagan, I firmly believe, "The best social program is a job." But it is more than that. It is the pursuit of happiness. It is being able to provide for your family. It is the promise of a future. That is why my own life's work has been about helping people succeed.

For more than four decades, I have seen lives drastically changed by just one job. I have had the great privilege to be a part of real-life stories like the ones you will find in this book—where extraordinary men and women saw a big opportunity in even the smallest of jobs. I truly believe every job is an opportunity, a chance to make something of yourself, to better your life.

I hope the people in this book inspire you as much as they have me. May their stories give you hope.

Robert A. Funk
CEO, President, and Chairman of the Board,
Express Employment Professionals

ACKNOWLEDGMENTS

This book would not have been possible without the help of many people.

We would especially like to thank the men and women who shared their personal stories within the pages of this book. We are grateful to the many Express associates, staff members, franchisees, and International Headquarters employees who contributed valuable time and information.

We would also like to thank Jennifer Anderson and Sherry Kast, APR, for their work in managing the project, and Dale R. Lewis Agency for writing and compiling the stories. Special thanks to Brie Hobbs, Heather Koontz, and Kenny Reinbold for editing and to the following photographers and agencies:

Barclay Horner

Bellissimo Photography

Brian Cowen Photography

Carol Hansen Photography, LLC

Contemporary Photography

Dan Iott Photography

Daniel Sheehan Photography

David DuPuy Photography and Videography

Don Dickson Photography

Ed Clark Photography, Inc.

Jay Lindgren

Jenny Aubreu Photography

Jim Stafford Photography

Jerry Poppenhouse

Lindsay Wogen Photography

Mike Lewis Photography

Rich Morgan Photography

Robin Gaucher Photography

Roger Wyan Photography

Stephanie Davis Studio

Studio Duda LLC.

Studio L Photography

Sunset Studios, LLC

THEIR
QUOTES

I love the people I'm working with, but if I need another job or something happens to the company I'm working for now, I'm sure Express will help me out.

– Pedro Guerrero, Express Associate –

I get to see lives changed.
I have a purpose along with a career.

– Joe Paquette, Express Employee –

This has been my career for the last 18 years, and I still like getting up and going to work each morning.

– Mark Hagen, Express Franchisee –

For some, coming to Express is like going to the hospital.
They come here in pain. They come here as a last resort.
They are at their lowest moment,
and we are able to offer them hope.
– Rocky Gill, Express Franchisee –

To get the news that your employer is going to lay off
thousands of people and close the whole thing down,
you've really got to have faith in God at times like that.
– Jonathan Groeger, Express Associate –

It makes me happy to know he has had a better life
and a steady income for all these years
because we believed in him.
– Christy Taylor, Express Franchisee –

I want to give them the opportunities I didn't have
growing up. I want them to have paths
to whatever careers they want.
– Roberta Long, Express Associate –

*I've seen grown men cry because they've lost their jobs
and they have families to care for. We place them in jobs
and the next time we see them so happy, so relieved, so
grateful for the opportunity to work.*

– Pat Camp, Express Franchisee –

You do what you have to do.

– Dawn Yengich, Express Associate –

*Finally, we found one lady who agreed
to go to work for those two days.
The company loved her and hired her full time.*

– Deidra Viney, Express Franchisee –

*All I can say is that when someone needs a job I tell them
to try Express because I've found, even in rough times,
Express will get you working.*

– Tina Padilla, Express Associate –

THEIR
STORIES

---

*A compilation of stories
about Express employees, associates,
and franchisees, and the
hope that jobs provide.*

Janice Andrick
Against All Odds

In the 1950s, public school systems in the United States were not designed to meet the needs of children with even minor physical disabilities, let alone a child who was a quadriplegic.

Janice Andrick was born with cerebral palsy and was unable to use her arms or legs. At the age of one, she was a perfect candidate to attend the Capper Foundation for Crippled Children in Topeka, Kansas, on an outpatient basis.

Founded by former Kansas Governor and U.S. Senator Arthur Capper in 1920, the Capper Foundation provides physical, speech, and occupational therapy as well as educational training for students in kindergarten through high school.

As a young girl, Janice developed an early love for reading and as she grew older, it became apparent at Capper that she was a quick learner. This early education, psychological support, and training gave Janice the hope that, in spite of physical limitations, she would one day be able to work a regular job and enjoy the camaraderie of fellow workers. More than anything she wanted the same fulfillment her sister and brothers were experiencing in their jobs.

Following the completion of her basic educational training, Janice went to work in the sheltered workshop at Capper. In order to work elsewhere, Janice and others with physical disabilities had to overcome great roadblocks. The Individuals with Disabilities Education Act (IDEA) ensuring that children with disabilities receive public education wasn't enacted until 1975 and even after the law passed, those ready to enter the workforce found it was difficult convincing employers to give them a chance.

Janice was in her early 30s when the Americans with Disabilities Act of 1990 was signed into law. She continued to learn and persevere, paving the way for a better future, not only for herself, but for others with disabilities as well.

Through Express Employment Professionals, she found a position doing clerical work for the State of Kansas Department of Disability Services. With the advancement in computer technology, Janice saw her opportunities increase and became a computer data entry specialist with the assistance of ongoing training offered by Express. She became very skilled in the use of a tool known as a head stick, and a master of a communication board, allowing her to speak out about her ideas to supervisors and co-workers regarding how the jobs they performed could be improved.

With the aid of these technologies, the inclusion that Janice sought for so long had at last been achieved.

Now Janice uses her communication board to visit with the many friends she made during her career that spanned more than 20 years. Though much of her life has been a struggle, she has loved every minute of the time she has spent working and being considered "just one of the gang." And if pressed, she might confide the only thing she enjoys more than her former career, or listening to an old recording of Elvis, is cheering on "her" Kansas Jayhawks.

Meghan Andryski
A Heart for Others

Meghan Andryski's grandmother worked as a transcriptionist translating books, newspaper articles, and other materials into braille for the blind. So as a child, Meghan learned braille as easily as most children learn their ABCs. Little did Meghan know the time spent with her grandmother would shape her college career and equip her to be a perfect candidate for a company that provides products for people with disabilities.

Growing up in Plymouth, Minnesota, Meghan was also extremely active in sports. She was the team captain on her school's varsity diving team and competed in gymnastics. When she went to college, she started out studying kinesiology, how muscles move and interact. Along the way, her goals changed and she became an interpreter for the deaf and blind. She earned an associate of applied science degree in sign language, interpretation, and transliteration from St. Paul College and then went on to the University of Minnesota where she served as a sign language tutor while earning a bachelor's degree in communications. After graduation, she worked at the Intermediate District 287 School for five years, aiding special education teachers by teaching life skills, goal setting, and independence to the visually and hearing impaired students.

In January 2013, Meghan had a life-changing experience when she tripped and fell on ice, shattering her entire leg, both the tibia and the fibula. She had several surgeries and couldn't put any weight on her leg or even have it in a vertical position because of swelling. "I had one of the worst breaks the doctors had seen," she said. "While I was healing, I had lots of time to think about life, and where I had been and where I was going. That's when I decided it was time to change my career path."

Meghan's initial contact with Express Employment Professionals took place soon after her recovery. She heard Express was interested in finding people to help individuals with disabilities. After meeting with Meghan, the Express staff told her about a job opening in Eden Prairie, a suburb of Minneapolis, with a company serving the hearing impaired and blind communities. The company provides tools and technology for people with disabilities from flashing alarms for fire, carbon monoxide, and weather alerts, to vibrating alarm clocks and amplified telephones for the hard of hearing.

"I went in for the interview and was hired on the spot," Meghan said. "Even though accepting the job meant moving away from St. Paul, I was really excited about the opportunity. I have a lot of knowledge about both the deaf and blind communities, especially how they interact with others."

Meghan's skills and her heart for helping people were a perfect fit for the job. From her first day on the job, Meghan felt right at home helping customers with their purchasing decisions. Since a significant amount of orders come in via Skype, many of the company's customer representatives are fluent in sign language.

"I look back at the way things have all worked out for me, and I realize that these people come in here or contact us electronically hoping to find help," Meghan said. "Since I am trained in sign language and braille, I can be the person who helps these people create a bridge between two worlds."

Mary Bailey
Finding One's Place in the World

Waking up wanting to go to work every day, and enjoying her job, co-workers, and adopted "kids" are some of the perks of Mary Bailey's career.

The former convenience store operator, church facilities manager, and all-around hard worker, Mary finally found her niche at Independence Community College (ICC) in Kansas and credits Express Employment Professionals for finding her the perfect job.

Mary and her husband ran convenience stores for years before getting out of the business in 2009. Mary then went to work for her church as a facilities manager.

"After about a year, I realized I needed some health insurance badly but I couldn't afford it and the jobs I worked didn't offer benefits," she said.

"A friend knew I wasn't happy, so she suggested I talk to her niece who worked at Express and see if there was anything available," Mary said. "I went in and took the test that they have for you. They're good about asking questions to pair you up with a line of work you would like and be good at."

Mary was quickly matched with an opening at ICC, working part time as the athletic director's assistant.

"I filled in for the athletic department and absolutely fell in love with it," Mary said. "I enjoyed working with the students and the coaches. Luckily, when my original assignment ended, they kept me on part time working in the dorms."

While working 20 hours in the dorms, Mary picked up another assignment from Express to work an additional 20 hours at the school's welcome desk. Then a position opened up for a student life coordinator planning activities for students, leading student groups, and getting campus organizations up and running. Mary applied and was hired as a permanent employee of the college.

"I'm basically the 'dorm mom,'" she said. "So I tell the kids when they come in, they're mine. Good, bad, and ugly, I'll be here for them."

Mary acts as an advocate for students if they have a problem with an instructor, coach, or fellow student. She is proud to say that she has also helped implement some new things at ICC.

"We signed on with the University of Kansas for a telemedicine program to offer our kids free counseling," Mary said. "They can check out an iPad which allows them to receive counseling in their rooms privately if they need it."

Under Mary's keen direction, a care team was developed on campus so that more people will be involved in looking out for the welfare of individual students when they need help. Student government has also been reinstated. And, Mary created the Campus Activities Board so that students have more of a say in the university's organized activities.

"My goal is to make a difference in these kids' lives and I do my best to take care of them just like they were my own," Mary said.

"It was just amazing because the first assignment Express sent me on was to ICC and I got the job, and have basically been here ever since. I am very blessed. I absolutely enjoy my job. I can't imagine not being here."

Josh Baughman
Following His Dreams

Josh Baughman grew up around Express Employment Professionals. From when he was eight years old until he was 11, his mom worked in an Express office, so Josh would come by every day after school. Before long, he was running errands, working the copy machine, hangin' out with the office workers, and chatting with job applicants who were waiting for appointments. Little did Josh realize that the relationship with Express would continue through the years.

Josh was raised in Odessa, Texas, and when he turned 16 it was natural for him to look to Express for temporary jobs in the summer. During the school year, he was busy with sports and lettered in football throughout high school. But once football season was over, he found after-school jobs through Express. Even when he went to college, Express helped Josh find part-time jobs to cover some of his expenses.

But, after only one year of college, Josh chose to go to work full time instead of completing his degree. "Sometimes I think that was a good idea. Sometimes I think it wasn't, but that was the road I chose," he said.

At age 22, Josh decided to open his own business. "I own a sandblasting company in Odessa. We sandblast drilling rigs and gas pipes and do all kinds of industrial sandblasting."

As Josh began to get his business rolling, he went to Express for his workforce needs.

"If I need five or six employees as temporaries or full-time employees, I go to Express," he said. "Right now, I have 35 people working for me, so business is doing really well."

Today, at the age of 25, Josh is already a successful businessman. He is married to a school teacher and has a five-year-old son and a three-year-old daughter. Josh's goal is to provide for his family in the same way his dad did for him and his brother.

"My dad was always motivated to make sure we never wanted for anything," Josh said. "That's my motivation now. I want my children to have whatever they need in their lives and to make the right choices."

Josh's booming business allows him to follow his dream. He's also an avid racer for the American Sprint Car Series (ASCS), traveling to races throughout the country 35 to 40 weekends a year. He drives number 17, a Baughman Motorsport winged sprint car. "For me, racing is more than just a hobby. I love it and do it as often as I can."

As busy as he is with family, business, and racing, Josh still drops by the Express office in Odessa whenever he can to see his friends. "I've continued to have a good relationship with everyone who works there. They're a great company, and that's why we've stuck with them as long as we have," Josh said. "Express certainly helped me get where I am now."

Jim Britton
Helping People Succeed

Aside from seven years in the restaurant business, Jim Britton has spent his entire career in staffing, and it has been a perfect match for him.

Born in Springfield, Illinois, Jim grew up in a subdivision just three miles west of the city. He graduated from Pleasant Plains Community High School in a class of only 30 students. After earning his degree in business administration from Western Illinois University, he ran his own Italian restaurant franchise, but was ready for a change.

Jim realized that many businesses such as grocery stores, department stores, restaurants, and real estate offices fell into two categories: "Mom and Pop" stores or national chains. He wanted to be affiliated with a company that had a national presence and offered support far beyond what an individual could provide for themselves.

"My wife and I were still quite young and had three children ages three, six, and nine when we invested our entire life savings in 1980 into a franchise with then Acme Personnel. When I acquired my franchise, I remember Bob Funk, a vice president at Acme then, picking me up at the Oklahoma City airport in a yellow Cadillac Eldorado," Jim said.

Three years after Jim opened his office, Acme's president passed away quite suddenly, and the company went into bankruptcy.

Although Acme went out of business, Jim and his wife, Carole, continued working in the staffing industry as independent owners. At the same time, Bob along with two other business associates from Acme, purchased several franchises of Acme which later became Express Employment Professionals.

Jim stayed in contact with Bob. Then in 1986, Bob arranged a meeting with Jim to encourage him to buy an Express franchise and become a Regional Developer for the newly formed staffing company.

"Looking to the future, I decided I could go further faster, and with greater security, with someone other than just myself," Jim said.

Twenty-eight years later, Jim has never looked back on his decision. "So much of the success I've been able to enjoy is because of the people I've surrounded myself with, from team members who work for us and with us, to the people at Express International Headquarters who help us navigate both the changes in our industry and in the national economy," Jim said.

As a successful business person and franchise owner, Jim's goal is to develop people in terms of their knowledge, skills, and enthusiasm for the business. He enjoys helping people succeed, whether they are job seekers or potential franchise owners. It is obvious that Jim is very proud of his accomplishments when it comes to developing his staff and fellow franchisees.

"Express has many, many success stories of people who come in the door in a fragile or frightened condition, and walk out with a place to go to work," Jim said.

Wakina Buxton-Frazier
A Relay to Success

Originally from New Jersey, Wakina Buxton-Frazier began working early in life. At just 16, she got her first job while also completing high school.

Wakina attended college for a while, but her primary focus was on finding a job that would help her gain experience and build a career. Wakina found herself moving from one job to another, from nonprofit to the corporate sector. She enjoyed the challenges of the varied settings, and established a solid core of office and administrative skills. Eventually, Wakina decided she wanted a change of pace and relocated from the high-pressure, fast-moving lifestyle of New Jersey and settled in Atlanta, Georgia.

In Atlanta, Wakina learned that many large companies built their workforces through staffing companies. Always seeking the opportunity for continued growth and success, she began working with Express Employment Professionals in the Atlanta Mid-Town office. That's where she met her hero and mentor, owner Calvin Green. Along with what she calls "tough love," Calvin provided Wakina with encouragement and backing.

"He always tries to push people to be their best," Wakina said. "He believed in me and put in the effort to help me reach my goals. He always stood behind my career development 100 percent."

She told her mentor that, first and foremost, she was looking for stability and a chance to grow. She was tired of moving from job to job, whether it was because of relocating, a challenging economy, or a company closing.

Right away, Express found a job for her as a receptionist. Although Wakina's skills and experience made her overqualified for the position, Calvin told her that the company was solid and offered chances to move up if she proved herself.

Wakina trusted his advice and took the job. She worked hard to establish herself as a reliable professional and accepted any new responsibility that was offered to her. When another employee left, she was offered that job. Settling into that company made Wakina feel like a burden had been lifted from her shoulders.

Today, she enjoys her job and looks forward to new opportunities within the company. "I feel stable, and I have an opportunity to grow with this company," she said.

Wakina's quick to credit Express for not only finding her a good job with potential, but also for the hard work in supporting and encouraging her.

"I'm very grateful to Express. Without them I wouldn't be in this job," Wakina said.

In addition to her full-time job, she is also working on opening her own small business in her spare time. She's determined that the skills she's learned in building a stable career can also be used to help other people.

"My overall goal is to be a success story...to leave a legacy," she said.

Randall and Pat Camp
In God's Time

With their Christian faith and marriage binding them together, Randall and Pat Camp always rely on God to direct their business decisions.

Randall grew up working in the family's meat packing company where he eventually became part owner. His clients were "Mom and Pop" grocers and when the big grocery store chains began to push the smaller stores out of business, Randall and his brother, Dennis, made the difficult decision to sell the family business. He continued to work with the new owners as a consultant for a couple of years.

Randall then got a sales job with a company in Atlanta. "The company eventually wanted us to transfer to Atlanta, which meant uprooting from our hometown of Ocala," Pat said. "Our children were teenagers at the time and we just couldn't agree to that idea at all. So all of a sudden, Randall was unemployed."

At the time, Pat was a registered nurse, working long hours to make ends meet. It was a very difficult time for both of them and it soon became clear that Randall wanted to own a business again. He began researching business opportunities and right away, the couple zeroed in on Express Employment Professionals. When they learned that the Express office in Ocala was for sale, they thought their prayers had been answered. However, another couple was already trying to buy that franchise territory. "We were devastated," Pat said. "It blew the wind out of our sails because we were so sure that this office was meant to be ours. We began to explore other avenues and began negotiations with another staffing company, but our hearts really weren't in it."

The Camps called the couple who had just bought the Express office to see how they were doing and let them know they were going to start giving them some friendly competition.

The other couple confided that they were very unhappy, missing the lawn care business they had been in before and had figured out that the employment business was not a good fit for them. Randall and Pat immediately purchased their franchise. "It was an answer to our prayer!" Pat said. "We were ecstatic that the Lord had worked all this out in His own time."

Helping people find work has been fulfilling for the Camps. "It is just heart-wrenching sometimes, seeing people come in so desperate for work," Pat said. "I've seen grown men cry because they've lost their jobs and they have families to care for. We place them in jobs and then the next time we see them so happy, so relieved, so grateful for the opportunity to work."

Because of their success, the Camps have implemented other ways to help people they encounter. "Randall, I, and others on staff put donations each month into what we call 'the pot.' When we hear about a need, whether it's for groceries, to pay an electric bill, or to replace a broken-down car, that money can be used to fill the need."

The Ocala office also has a corporate chaplain. "This person is here for our clients, our associates, and our own staff as well," Pat said. "Anytime anyone needs counseling, he can help us right away. One time, one of our clients was on the verge of a divorce. We offered him this counseling service free of charge, and the chaplain helped that couple put their marriage back together."

When not running their business, the Camps enjoy relaxing on the beach, visiting grandchildren, and counting their blessings. They're looking forward to many, many more years, all the while putting their business in God's hands.

Amy Clegg
From Junior Achievement to Successful Owner

Born in Scranton, Pennsylvania, Amy Clegg was the youngest of six children in her family. Amy's childhood summers were spent in the Poconos swimming and hanging out at the resorts in the area. In the fall and spring, she attended Catholic school and became involved in Junior Achievement during high school. "We started our own business and learned first-hand about running a company," Amy said. "I was so involved as a leader in Junior Achievement that I began going to the grade schools to teach children about the business world. Years later, as a business owner, I continued to volunteer at grade schools, presenting about free enterprise and how to get a good job."

After college, Amy worked for a staffing company in the Poconos. Seven years later, the franchisees of that company went their own ways. The former franchisor told her he believed she had the potential to own a business, so he gave Amy the funding for one year to help her get started. Not surprisingly, at the end of the year Amy was on her own two feet. A few years later, she invested in a second office back in her hometown of Scranton and everything looked rosy.

But Amy and her husband had a personal obstacle to overcome. They dearly wanted children and decided to adopt a little boy from Vietnam and a little girl from Kazakhstan. Within a couple of years they had the family they wanted but life became much more hectic. With two little ones at home, Amy decided to simplify things and sell the Poconos office so she could concentrate on her Scranton office.

In 2008, a friend and former employee who worked at the Express office in the Poconos told Express about Amy and her independent office in Scranton. Before long, Express was calling her, hoping she would join the team.

"I gave them a really hard time," Amy said. "I asked them why in the world would I want to team with someone else and change our culture? I was very hands-on about my staffing business and I didn't think there would be any advantage for me to join Express."

So Amy did some investigating, some thinking, and some soul searching, and finally signed as an Express franchisee.

"Not long after I signed with Express, it became clear that I'd made the best business decision ever," Amy said. "In 2010, my first full year with them, my business grew 10 times its size. By teaming with Express, I have been able to help more people find work and more companies find great employees than I could ever have done as an independent."

As busy as she is, Amy still considers every associate special. One of her favorite stories is about a woman named Inge who came in needing a job badly.

Amy placed her as the housekeeper for the owners of a large manufacturing company. During the years, Amy and Inge stayed in contact until it came time for Inge to retire. "At that point, I asked Inge to move in with us," Amy said. "I had the two older children and a baby on the way, so I needed help with my own family. Even today, Inge is still part of our family, serving as a trusted caregiver for our children."

After joining Express, Amy and her team have grown and become known as staffing leaders and experts in their market. "Now, we look back at the thousands of people we've helped find work, and we feel so good. Today, I'm really happy I joined the Express family. Sometimes I shudder to think how close I came to walking away from this opportunity."

Mary Ann Cummings
Working on Her Own Terms

Mary Ann Cummings was born at home in Carbondale, Kansas, and raised on a farm with two sisters. She married at age 18 and her life with her husband, Frank, was anything but traditional. She worked, he didn't, and they were both fine with that. Mary Ann says that the arrangement was baffling to other people but completely natural to the two of them.

"In that era it was not acceptable for a man not to work," she said. "Frank often told people, 'She makes the living and I make the living worthwhile.'"

Mary Ann enjoyed a long-time career in state government. In 1965, Mary Ann began working for the State of Kansas Social and Rehabilitation Services, where she stayed for 18 years serving as secretary to the director of Children and Youth Programs. In 1983, she transferred to the Kansas Department of Health and Environment where she was the assistant to the Secretary until her retirement in 2000.

But, the self-professed workaholic, Mary Ann, really wasn't ready to just collect a retirement check, she wanted to continue working. And that's when Express Employment Professionals came through with a job that provided the flexibility she desired.

Mary Ann tried another temp agency, which required her to take a "long, drawn-out test" in order to place her in a job. Frustrated with the process, Mary Ann would have none of it. She came highly recommended with glowing letters about her character and "tremendous working knowledge" of state government. Mary Ann's outstanding employee performance evaluations also praised her effectiveness and dedication.

"I said, 'you know, I can write a letter and I can spell, and I can add two and two, and if you can't find something for me without taking some four-hour test, forget it,'" she said.

She went to Express, where, after a "little, abbreviated test" online, she was placed right away—and wound up working for the same agency from which she had retired.

Through Express, she returned to the Kansas State Department of Health and Environment. She is charged with data entry and performing background checks on potential employees. The transition was an easy one for Mary Ann.

"Express is the best employer I've ever had. I go in and get my paycheck and I never have any issues with them," Mary Ann said. "I let them know my availability and when I need time off. So far that's been okay and I love the flexibility."

The flexible schedule allows her to take off regularly to visit her grandchildren in Arkansas. She is happy to go to work and finish her job, whether it means working eight hours in a day—or not.

"At this point in my life, I like the idea that I am not a traditional employee," Mary Ann said. "And, thanks to Express I'm working because that's all I've ever done."

Greg and Rina Donaldson
A Quarter Century of Success

Greg Donaldson and his wife, Rina, have been the owners of the Bozeman, Montana, Express Employment Professionals office for 25 years, and they've loved every minute of it.

Rina started her career working with senior citizens in recreation therapy. When Rina married Greg, he was a salesman and was traveling quite a bit, so once they had kids she stayed home with them for several years.

Greg then went to work for Express. The owner of the Bozeman Express office at that time had quite a few other business enterprises to run, so he hired Greg to come in and manage the office for him. Within a couple of months, he asked the Donaldsons if they wanted to purchase the franchise.

"I never will forget that day," Rina said. "It was a golden opportunity and quite a good deal. Buying the franchise so early in its establishment meant it was very affordable. The area had not been worked yet, so we jumped at the chance. That was in 1988, and here we are 25 years later."

Throughout the years, Greg and Rina have been pushed to learn and grow the business. Coming into the computer and technological age was a challenge, and the ups and downs of the economy always impact their operations.

"Greg and I make a great team because we recognize one another's gifts. He is an amazing salesman, and I am a great office person. We complement each other. Being an entrepreneur is Greg's dream, and being alongside him is my dream," she said.

Now, their goal is to continue to build their business up after the most recent recession, as well as continue an active lifestyle by hiking and camping throughout the beautiful state of Montana.

Even after 25 years, Rina still loves doing what she does. "We are hope-givers," she said. "That's how we think of ourselves. Every day we provide hope for people coming to us, desperate for jobs.

"One of my favorite stories is about Eric Urban. He was trying to get his degree in fish and game management here in Bozeman when tragedy struck his family," Rina said. "Eric came to us so traumatized that he couldn't face people at all. His therapist actually told him to try to get a temporary job to ease himself back into the workforce, so he came to us for help, and now, he is going back to college. I think that is impressive, and his whole story is so inspiring to us. We were glad we could help him through that hard time."

We are hope-givers. That's how we think of ourselves. Every day we provide hope for people coming to us, desperate for jobs.

Greg and Rina have story after story of how they've helped people along the way. "Success stories like Eric's make all the work worth it," Rina said. "Employment is a big deal in people's lives, and when they don't have a job, things can get pretty grim. I've seen it again and again, a job can turn a life around."

Garrett Fairbanks
Putting One Foot in Front of the Other

Garrett Fairbanks found himself homeless and unemployed, carrying a bag on his back and selling aluminum scrap just to put some money in his pocket. But Garrett didn't let the difficult circumstances push him into deep despair. Instead, he told himself to keep stepping forward.

Garrett grew up in Kenosha, Wisconsin, with his parents and two brothers. He recalls good years playing outdoor sports and singing in the high school choir. When he got out of school, he started working but during the recession, he was laid off.

He started collecting unemployment and tried his hand at home repair and odd jobs but couldn't find enough work to support himself.

His housing situation was also unstable. Before long Garrett didn't have the money for an apartment of his own, so he stayed with friends, bouncing around from place to place. And then, his unemployment benefits ran out.

"I didn't have the money to really pay for anything, so I had to move out of my friend's house," he said. "It got rough for a while. I was pretty much on the streets, carrying a bag on my back, basically homeless."

Garrett got involved with a church program, which offered him housing each night at a different church. As part of the program, he was required to actively search for work and take part in different job coaching classes, like résumé preparation.

"The program got me moving a little quicker, helping put my name out there," Garrett says. "That's when I ended up finding Express."

Garrett filled out an application with Express and went in for an interview. Within a week he was hired as a machinist for a local manufacturing company. "Express found the job rather quickly and got me where I needed to go," Garrett said.

But when it came to getting to his new job each day, Garrett was on his own. He did not have a vehicle, so he set out on a five to six mile bicycle ride each morning—as early as 6 a.m. from the different churches where he was staying, and in all kinds of weather.

Three months later, things continued to get better for Garrett as he was hired on permanently. He also received assistance in getting an apartment.

Having a job changed my life.

Garrett says things are very different in his life now. He is proud to be financially stable, living in his own apartment and paying his bills.

"Life is good," he said. "I'm just trying to do the best I can. Not everything is perfect but I'm getting there. I can afford to do things on my own which really means something to me. If I want to go out to dinner one night, I can do that instead of having to worry, 'Where am I going to eat next?' or 'Where am I going to sleep?'"

Garrett was recognized as the 2012 Wisconsin Employee of the Year by Express for his dedication and inspirational rags-to-riches story.

"Things changed quickly," he said. "I went from being homeless to having my own apartment and a good job. Having a job changed my life."

Rocky Gill
Second and Third Chances

Born in Tyler, Texas, Rocky Gill moved 10 times during his childhood because of his father's job as a salesman. As a result, Rocky decided when he finished college he would settle somewhere and stay there the rest of his life. In 1981, after graduating from a private Christian college in Chattanooga, Tennessee, with an accounting degree, Rocky moved back to Tyler. His grandmother, who lived there, set him up with an interview at a CPA firm which promptly offered him a job.

Rocky later became a controller for a health care organization. This was a great career, but Rocky wondered whether he might find a better fit owning a business. "I worked hard and took my job personally," Rocky said. "The trouble was that I was just on a salary, so I wasn't being compensated for my extra efforts. I began to think it might make sense if I could find some way to work for myself."

A friend of his opened an Express Employment Professionals office and started telling Rocky about the advantages of being an Express franchisee. "Before I knew it, my friend arranged for me to go to headquarters in Oklahoma City for what Express calls Discovery Day," Rocky said. "I found myself being shown around the office. I didn't know it at the time but the company leaders were evaluating me to see if I'd fit into the Express family. Since I had not realized what this event was all about, I had not prepared financially to make a buying decision. The company leaders must have sensed my insecurities because at the end of Discovery Day, I wasn't offered a franchise."

For Rocky, this was a difficult time. He had loved Express from the moment he walked in the door. "The whole feel of the place emanated with excitement, integrity, and positive energy.

I was especially impressed with CEO Bob Funk. I could tell he was an extraordinary man who had built a fantastic team of people around him. I knew then that this was the kind of company I wanted to be associated with."

Two years later, Rocky had another chance, but a different obstacle arose. A verbal commitment was given to a neighboring franchisee saying his territory could include Tyler. That news was extremely disappointing for Rocky.

However, the other franchisee changed his mind, deciding he didn't want Tyler as part of his territory. "Needless to say, I went right back for the next Discovery Day and was accepted for a franchise," Rocky said.

After 18 years as an Express franchisee, Rocky has his share of stories to tell. One associate who stands out in his mind is a lady named Sue who came in upset because she had just been fired from her job as a bookkeeper. As Sue told her story to Rocky, her eyes filled with tears and Rocky's heart went out to her.

Determined to help, the office called the health care company where Rocky once worked, and it turned out they needed someone in admitting. Sue ended up working for that company for 15 years and only recently retired.

"Sue's story caught my attention and captured my heart, but there are so many stories like hers," Rocky said. "For some people, coming to Express is like going to the hospital. They come in here in pain. They come in as a last resort. They are at their lowest moment, and we are able to offer them hope."

In addition to helping people find jobs, Rocky loves spending time with his granddaughter and playing the piano.

Chris Green
More Than He Dared to Imagine

Chris Green was 20 years old when he first learned about Express Employment Professionals. For two years Chris balanced work while taking part-time courses at a local junior college in Fort Worth, Texas. In 1998, he was feeling the difficulty of this balance and made the commitment to get ahead in life. He wasn't sure what he needed to do, but he knew he had to do something.

Chris found an advertisement for Express in the newspaper and gave them a call. They told him they would be happy to schedule an interview. And although it didn't take long for Express to find a placement for Chris, he had already found a job on his own, loading trucks at a shipping company in Dallas. It only took Chris two weeks to know that the job was not what he wanted. He called the Fort Worth Express office back and asked if the job they had found for him was still available. They told him it was. In fact, they told Chris he could start work the very next morning.

He went to work for a small company of about 40 people where he programmed data into mobile phones. After 90 days Chris was hired full time into the direct fulfillment area as part of the company's programming group. His job was to gather specific information such as the customer phone number and the coverage area the customer needed, as well as the features required. Once all this data was gathered, Chris would set up the phone service.

Hard work and attention to detail would continue to pay off for Chris during his career. Chris was promoted to team leader, and soon thereafter, he found himself promoted to coordinator and later to supervisor.

With the sudden increase in cell phone use in the U.S., the department he supervised grew from eight to 15 associates. Even with his expanded crew, the growth was so rapid that at one point they worked 12-16 hour shifts for more than a month without a single day off.

Chris continued to acquire new skills on the job. He was learning new procedures, technologies and systems at work. And the promotions kept coming. Two years later, a merger and another surge in business volume brought another promotion for Chris as he was named manager. Then in May 2011, at age 33, Chris was promoted to director.

He had started out as a temporary employee with a company of 40 workers and he now oversees 700 line workers, five managers, and 22 supervisors.

As the company has expanded through the years, Chris continues to work with Express for his hiring needs.

He had started out as a temporary employee with a company of 40 workers and now he oversees 700 line workers, five managers, and 22 supervisors.

Jonathan Groeger
Faith, Patience, and Persistence

Upon hearing the news that the New Orleans shipyard where Jonathan Groeger worked was set to close, he desperately began looking for work. He sent out résumés anywhere and everywhere.

Just when Jonathan felt like he wasn't having any luck with his job search, he received a call from a professional recruiter with Express Employment Professionals. That call changed Jonathan's outlook.

Express had a machine shop client looking for an engineer and they needed to hire someone as soon as possible. The recruiter called to discuss the position and set up an interview that same day with Jonathan.

"To my surprise, not long after I arrived at the interview, they were saying the job is here—do you want it?" Jonathan said. "It was the perfect job for me because I love working in a machine shop. Taking a raw product and turning it into a finished one—with so much detail, so much thought going into it, and seeing it come to fruition—is very gratifying."

After seven months on the job, Jonathan was hired on full time.

Jonathan grew up in the small town of Denham Springs, Louisiana. Both his father, a pipe fitter, and his mother, a nurse, taught him the value of hard work and achieving one's goals.

"My parents always taught me to work for what I want. My first purchase was a Super Nintendo," he said. "The deal was that my brother and I would come up with half the cost. We did, and my parents came up with the other half."

Growing up in a Christian household, his parents also taught him to have faith in God. "God's going to put you on the path that He has designed for you," Jonathan said. "To get the news that your employer is going to lay off thousands of people and close the whole thing down, you've really got to have faith in God at times like that."

He also recalls learning an important lesson of patience and persistence from his mom. In third grade, Jonathan asked his mother if he could play the saxophone. "She thought it was just a phase and told me if I still felt that way in a year, I'd get music lessons," he said.

Jonathan waited patiently. After a year had passed, he approached his mother again. "So, are we going to get saxophone lessons or what?" he asked.

He says the decision to take saxophone lessons influenced his life in ways he could not have imagined. He stuck with music and played the saxophone in junior high, high school, and college.

The persistence Jonathan had in playing the saxophone was the same persistence he relied upon to press forward in his job search. He also credits the Express recruiter for getting his career started at the machine shop. "Express was a crucial link between where I am now and where I was at the shipyard," he said. "If the recruiter hadn't found my résumé, I don't know where I'd be."

Pedro Guerrero
Keep on Truckin'

Pedro Guerrero is one hard-working man and, at the age of 61, he's still going strong. His can-do attitude has served him well from his teenage years to his post-military career.

"There I was, 16 years old and getting paid only 50 cents an hour working on car engines," Pedro said. "So I thought, diesel machines will be around forever. I'll go into the Army and let them train me to be a diesel mechanic. I joined the military in February 1969 and was trained on many things, but I never was assigned to be a mechanic."

The Army sent Pedro to Fort Carson, Colorado, and put him in the motor pool as a truck driver delivering boots, food, and supplies that the troops needed. "For me, I thought that was pretty cool," Pedro said. "I was 17 years old, and I was driving two-ton or five-ton vehicles all over."

Then when the war broke out, Pedro served in Vietnam. He was put in an artillery battery and assigned to a .50 caliber machine gun mounted on a truck. "I learned that if I could do this one thing, I could learn other things," he said.

Pedro now works as a machinist and he's willing to get more schooling any time the opportunity arises. "You need to be ready to work hard to improve yourself and you need to be willing to learn about computers if you want to keep up in this world," he said.

His skills and excellent work ethic paid off, especially at a time when he worried about losing his job. He was working in a shop where they were constantly laying people off. "They'd bring people in and then as soon as things got slow they'd let them go," Pedro said. "Then later, they'd hire a bunch more. I thought I would be next."

That's when Pedro met Maria Blackwell at Express Employment Professionals.

"The people at Express have been so helpful to me. Maria told me not to worry, that if I was laid off, she'd just go find me another job," he said. "When she said that, it made me happy.

"Another thing I like about Express is that they do their best to match whatever your qualifications are to the right job," Pedro said. "That's what happened with me. I didn't want to drive very far to get to work and back each day, so when I eventually got laid off Maria found me a new job that was close to my house. I love the people I'm working with, but if I need another job or something happens to the company I'm working for now, I'm sure Express will help me out."

Pedro plans to keep working into his 70s. And, when he retires he plans to enjoy time with his grandchildren. "I'll keep on doing whatever I can until the Lord says, that's enough. I want you to sit back and relax."

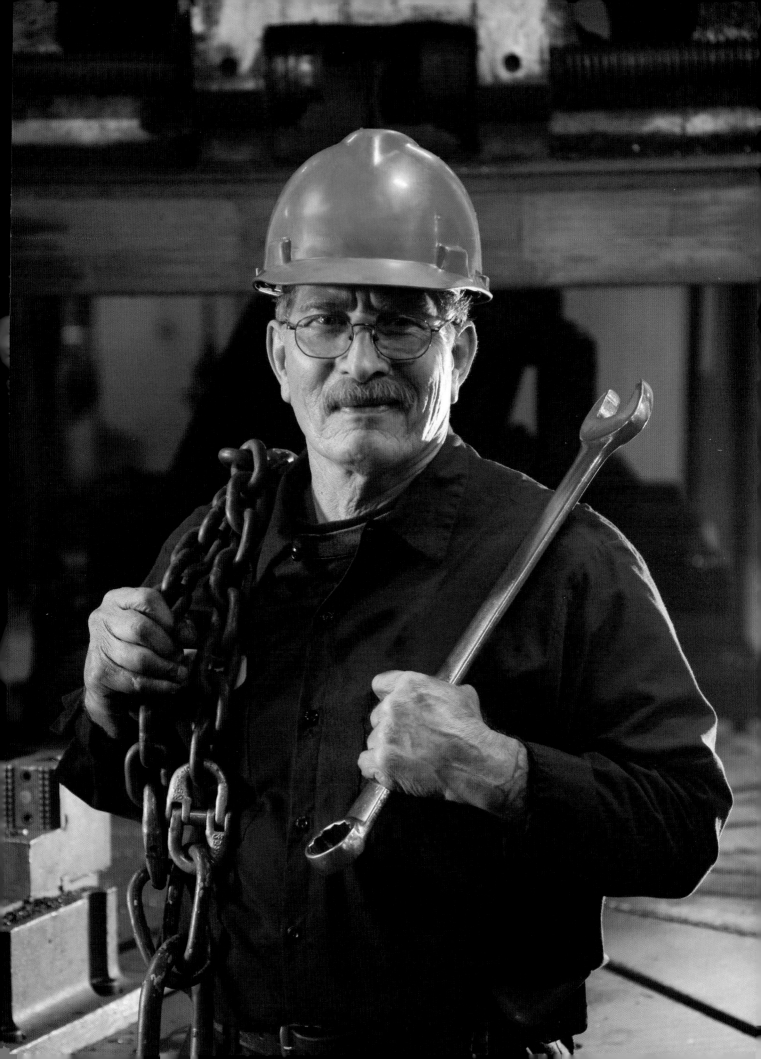

Mark and Sandy Hagen
The Value of a Good Mentor

Mark Hagen and his wife, Sandy, know the value of having a good mentor. They experienced first-hand how one person's advice can change your life forever. Now, Mark and Sandy enjoy what they do instead of dreading each work day.

Living in Seattle, Washington, Mark was a successful CPA and Sandy worked as a pharmacist. In 1996, Mark decided he wanted to do something else with his life, so he and Sandy began to chat with Ralph Palmen, who was a long-time friend of Mark's father. As it turned out, Ralph was a Regional Developer for Express Employment Professionals and had been part of the Express team since its beginning.

It didn't take long for Ralph to see that Mark and Sandy had the potential to become successful members of the Express family. According to Mark, "Ralph got us so excited about buying our own franchise that we both quit our jobs and uprooted ourselves from Seattle to move about an hour north to the much smaller community of Mount Vernon."

With Ralph's help, guidance, and wisdom, the Hagens soon had their business off to a great start, and they knew they could always go to him with questions or concerns.

"I fell in love with this business," Mark said. "I really enjoy working with job seekers to help them find work, and it is so much more enjoyable than crunching numbers as an accountant. This has been my career for the last 18 years, and I still like getting up and going to work each morning."

"Sandy loved me enough to move with me, and she has been a huge part of our success," Mark said. "Express likes to have husband and wife teams as franchise owners. I think it adds to the idea of us being a caring family for our clients. Sandy and I have had great staff members as we've watched our office grow. In 1998, we even bought a second franchise in Bellingham."

When asked how his life has improved since he and Sandy plunged into the staffing business, Mark said, "Financially, it has been great. I'm making more than I would have as a CPA, and I certainly have more control over my own future. Mostly, though, I like the feeling of helping people."

After Ralph changed their lives by mentoring them, Mark and Sandy have had numerous opportunities to pay it forward and help change other people's lives.

Mark recalls one particular gentleman who came into their office with a marginal work history, but he and Sandy both found the man's story compelling. They put him to work at a manufacturing company and when he made it through his evaluation period, the company hired him full time. Eventually, that company went out of business, so the Hagens lost contact with the gentleman. Three years later, that same fellow came back to the Express office to thank the Hagens for giving him a shot. The man revealed that he had actually been on the verge of taking his own life that fateful day when the Hagens gave him a job. "That's a story Sandy and I will not soon forget," Mark said.

Carrie Harmes has a love for learning. In high school, Carrie focused on academics, was a member of the National Honor Society, and graduated valedictorian. When Carrie attended the University of Louisiana in Lafayette she discovered a passion for photography, earning a Bachelor of Fine Arts degree in visual arts and photography. Unfortunately, jobs were hard to come by for photographers, so Carrie spent several years working in the food service industry.

Carrie later married and took some time off from work to raise a family. When Carrie's youngest child was less than two years old, Carrie returned to college and earned her MBA with a specialization in accounting from Colorado State University in Pueblo. She is now studying to become a certified public accountant.

Carrie's first big break occurred when she began searching for career opportunities online. In the spring of 2012, Carrie found several advertisements placed by Express Employment Professionals for positions in her field of accounting and financial services.

"I went in for an interview and Express took the time to match my talents and training with the skills their clients were looking for," Carrie said. "Even though I was fresh out of school and jobs were still tough to find, they found a really good fit for me with an excellent company. Then they followed up several times to make sure the placement was working out for both me and the employer.

"In my first position, I helped start a tax preparation service and that job was a springboard to a career with the same firm, assisting senior citizens with their estate planning. I am currently the office manager. In addition to my accounting responsibilities, I am looking forward to working on the development of a quarterly newsletter for our clients."

Working with Express has given Carrie's career a tremendous boost. They were able to find positions for her with companies she would not have had access to otherwise.

At this point, Carrie's primary career goal is to assist in the growth of the tax preparation and financial planning departments where she works as she pursues her CPA.

In her personal life Carrie cherishes the time she spends with her family. She loves the simple things they do together from planting a garden to playing in the backyard.

"I want to be a really good role model for my kids. I want to provide an example of achieving success, hard work, and self discipline but I also want them to know that it is equally important to be devoted to your family. Like everyone, I'm busy, but I know this time with the kids is short and I want to enjoy it as much as I can," Carrie said.

I want to be a really good role model for my kids. I want to provide an example of achieving success, hard work, and self discipline...

Ruben Herrera
Express Is Like Family

People often joke with Ruben Herrera, asking if there is anything he can't do.

While working a successful job at a local hospital, Ruben decided to also get a part-time job when his children headed off to college. He wanted to earn extra money to help put his kids through school. That's when he met the folks at Express Employment Professionals.

"I was so glad I discovered Express," he said. "I've done a little bit of everything for them. For 10 years, I took tickets at sporting events, and I loved that. I've done everything from catering to answering the phone, too."

"Ruben's personality, smile, and attitude are evident in his leadership style," said Veronica Zamora, who manages the Norman, Oklahoma Express office. "When I sent him on the first job he had great reviews, he was punctual, and the client absolutely loved him. They request Ruben every year. We don't have to worry about a thing with Ruben—and it's a guaranteed deal that the job is going to get done right."

Ruben has worked hard for his children and for Express. "There is a special bond with the whole team and Ruben. He's not just an associate, he is like family," Veronica said.

The feeling is mutual as Ruben also considers Express family. "They have a Christmas get-together each year and make sure everyone blends in and feels welcome," he said.

"You don't find people like Ruben," Veronica said. "He is genuine, trustworthy, 100 percent golden, and dependable. I can't stress how dependable he is. You need a project completed, he'll organize the project, taking the lead, and helping call fellow employees if they are late. Our projects are successful because of Ruben."

I was so glad
I discovered Express.

Now retired from his job at the hospital, Ruben spends some of his time volunteering. He was recently named volunteer of the year for the YMCA. And, he still works when Express calls him for an assignment. His temporary jobs now give him the flexibility to travel, giving him the opportunity to see his grandchild.

Ruben likes to stay busy, make new friends, and tell others about Express. "I just want to help people. If they are looking for a job, I tell them to try Express," he said. "They'll help you out. They'll even train you for a job if you need it."

Lindon Hibbert
A Passion for Cooking

Growing up with five brothers and five sisters, Lindon Hibbert's life adventure in the northwest parish of St. James on the tropical Caribbean island of Jamaica began with a passion to be a cook. He didn't want to do anything else.

In Jamaica, that means embracing flavors from the Arawak and Taino tribes along with Spanish, British, African, East Indian, and Chinese influences. In pursuit of his dream, Lindon spent much of his youth watching the technique of jerking, which is a method of slow cooking marinated meats and poultry over low flame smoke pits filled with pimento wood. Lindon spent time frequenting restaurants and hotel kitchens to observe the cooks.

In the early 90s, Lindon searched for a better economic future and left his native land, traveling to Brooklyn, New York, to follow his dream of attending culinary school. After seven years studying and working in New York, he moved to Florida still in pursuit of better opportunities.

Once in Florida, Lindon found Express. He walked into an Express Employment Professionals office in Port Charlotte, Florida, absolutely determined he would get a job. They provided him with several part-time positions which he accepted, all the while keeping an eye out for his perfect job. Then one day, Lindon learned of an opportunity that could be the gateway to fulfilling his life-long dream of becoming a cook. There was a job opening for a food service manager. But Lindon didn't meet the essential job requirements. He didn't have the computer skills.

Encouraged by the staff at Express, Lindon decided that he hadn't come this far to give up on his dream. He would develop the computer skills necessary to obtain the job. "Whatever my situation in life, I am prepared to deal with it," he said. "So I began to study."

Every day, after working his part-time job, Lindon went to the Express office to learn the required computer skills for the job. Lindon got the job and has served as the food service manager for three and a half years.

As for the future, Lindon said, "In whatever I do, the sky is the limit. That is what I reach for in my life."

In whatever I do, the sky is the limit.
That is what I reach for in my life.

Debbie Joswick
Finally Finding Fulfillment

Debbie Joswick now lives in Mount Vernon, Washington, but during her lifetime she has traveled the world. Born to a military family stationed in Yokohama, Japan, Debbie moved continuously during her childhood. After coming back to the United States, she lived everywhere from Maine to California.

At age 17, Debbie began her career as a horse trainer; showing, coaching, and judging horse shows throughout the U.S. She enjoyed her career, but after 25 years, she decided it was time to stop working with horses and get her bachelor's degree in electronic publishing. Unfortunately, after graduating she had trouble finding a job, so she went to a staffing agency for employment help. They worked to assist her, and before long she had her first position. From then on, whenever she moved to a new location, Debbie's first stop was the local Express office, and they always came through. She worked at a financial company, in the auto industry, and even at a law firm. However, no matter where she lived or how prestigious her position, her career was lacking something.

Six years ago, when Debbie moved to Mount Vernon she headed for the Express office to find a job, but this time fate had a major change in store for her.

"I was about to accept a position with a local company when I heard there was an opening in the Express office itself, so I applied for it, and the franchise owners gave me a shot," she said. "As soon as I started working for Express, I realized I had finally found what I'd been searching for. All those other jobs didn't offer me any type of fulfillment. At Express, I find fulfillment every day in helping people."

Debbie enjoys the challenge of multi-tasking, recruiting people to fill jobs, and working with clients to bring in new business. No two days are the same, and time never drags. The end result is that each day, Debbie knows she has accomplished something worthwhile.

"I love to get phone calls and emails from people telling us they would not have made it without us. One lady called to tell me she had found her own employment, which normally would be a bummer, but then she said, 'Deb, for three and a half years, you folks at Express kept groceries on the table for me, and I just want to say thank you.' That was so wonderful. When I know our office has found someone employment and I'm a part of that, it makes me feel good!"

I find fulfillment every day in helping people.

One feature of the Express family Debbie believes makes a huge difference is the fact that the franchises are all locally-owned. "When a staffing company has a corporate office in New York, each associate just becomes another number," she said. "With Express, we see each person as a member of our own community, so we want that person to succeed."

When Debbie isn't busy finding people jobs, she relaxes by going lake fishing up in the mountains about 15 minutes away from her home. "Being close to nature is so restful. If I catch some fish, that's just icing on the cake," she said. "Mostly, I just love being outdoors. Then I'm ready to get back to my fantastic job."

Heather Koontz and Evan Brazille
Supporting Each Other's Dreams

When Heather Koontz' brother, Evan Brazille, needed a job, she sent him to Express Employment Professionals, a company that's proven successful for her own job search.

As children, Heather and Evan lived in Amarillo, Texas. Then the family moved to Broken Arrow, Oklahoma. "I played viola in the high school orchestra and worked on the high school newspaper staff," Heather said. "At the University of Tulsa, I majored in film studies with a minor in creative writing. I had big dreams of writing the next blockbuster."

After graduation, Heather met her future husband, Byron, and moved to Oklahoma City to be closer to him. "When I moved, I was very worried about finding a job. It was a major life change, and I didn't have any work lined up," Heather said.

That's when she found Express Employment Professionals. Alongside Byron, Heather worked on a data entry contract for an energy company. When that contract ended, she noticed a post for a communications job at Express International Headquarters.

"Having worked with Express before, I knew it's where I needed to be," Heather said. "I applied right away."

Heather got that job and is currently working in Marketing and Communications. "I work with some of the most knowledgeable people in the business and I'm learning so much about this field. Right now, this is a temporary position, but I love working here so much I'm hoping the company will see me as an asset and hire me permanently."

When asked what she likes most about Express, she said, "The people at headquarters are wonderful and they truly mean it when they say they're trying to put a million people to work."

Evan is currently a sophomore at Oklahoma State University in Stillwater, majoring in mechanical engineering. When he began searching for a part-time job, Heather realized he needed some good advice. "I felt for him because he was going to school and had been out searching hard for a job," Heather said. "So I just told Evan to go to the Stillwater Express office."

When Evan walked into the Express office, he did not know what to expect. "The truth is that I wasn't real sure exactly what Express did. Then I realized that the company's whole reason for existence is to help folks find jobs – and they do it for free. I also appreciated the way the people there stick with you through the whole process. They treat you like you're supposed to be treated. I got a job just a couple of days after my interviews."

Through Express, Evan works in sales and support for an electronics company, and has even helped design some of their products. "I look forward to going to work because I like learning new things and having new experiences," he said. "Mostly, of course, I'm happy to have that paycheck arrive every week."

Together, Heather and Evan have done many things throughout the years, always supporting each other's dreams and goals. As kids, they would make fun videos and then show them to friends. They work so well as a team it's like they can read one another's minds. They've written film scripts together and have even done some camera work together. And today, they both enjoy working for Express.

Ask Terry Lampe who has been the most influential role model in his life and he will quickly tell you it's his father, Larry. Terry especially attributes his personal work ethic to him.

"When I was about 13, I wanted a mini bike. My dad told me I'd have to go to work to earn it," Larry said. "So I went to work for my dad and my uncle in the masonry business. And because I wanted that mini bike, I ended up being a bricklayer for about 28 years."

Following a lengthy career in the masonry business, Terry became tired of the feast or famine cycles in the brick laying industry. Due to seasonal changes, he would only work six months of the year and would be laid off during the winter months. He knew there had to be a better way to support his family and began to look for a job that would provide year-round employment so he could experience the security of a consistent income.

He saw an Express Employment Professionals advertisement in the local newspaper. Terry answered the ad and, almost immediately, Express found him a full-time job with a manufacturing company, where Terry worked for three and a half years building hydraulic systems for bleachers. When the manufacturing company began cutting back hours, he was laid off. Fortunately, Express quickly responded and helped him find another job within a week.

Terry currently serves as a warehouse lead for another manufacturing firm. He's been with this company for four and a half years and has proven to be one of their most reliable employees, and an indispensable part of their team.

"My goal is to continue to work my way up with this company so I have more security," Terry said. "I love my job and enjoy going in every day but I also know that if something happened Express would find me another position. I thank Express for helping me find a new career and a path to economic security."

When he is not working, his hobbies include target shooting, traveling, and restoring old cars. Terry is especially proud of a 1931 Desoto two-door coupe, which he has converted into a street rod.

My goal is to continue to work my way up with this company so I have more security.

Betsy Lindgren
Owning Her Destiny

Entrepreneurship runs in Betsy Lindgren's family. Born and raised in Wisconsin, Betsy knew from the start she wanted to own her own business. "My father is an entrepreneur. He was a pharmacist and had a string of drug stores," Betsy said. "So, I think it's in the blood."

For Betsy, it was not only the entrepreneurial spirit that drove her on her career path. It was also the opportunity to provide for her family. "I wanted to make sure I could give my children the same opportunities I was provided. I wanted to take them to Disney World because that's where they really wanted to go," Betsy said. She a was single mother with two daughters when she decided to take a risk by quitting her job and taking a loan out on her car to start her business.

Early in her career, Betsy began looking into the growing staffing industry for opportunities to run her own business. Her search led her to Express Employment Professionals. Already negotiating a contract with a different staffing company out of California, Betsy had a chance encounter with a Regional Developer for Express. The two had met once before, but Betsy had turned down the opportunity in an effort to pursue her other offer. "I had a ticket in my hand to hop on a plane to meet with the other staffing company when the Developer said, 'You owe me another meeting.'"

After meeting with the Express Developer and speaking with Express CEO, Bob Funk, Betsy's decision was made. "The next day, I was headed to Express International Headquarters in Oklahoma City," Betsy said. "On Monday, I was signing the contract. By Wednesday, I was back home planning the launch of my new business."

Betsy became the 27th Express franchise when she opened her Owatonna, Minnesota, office in 1985. Since then, she has become the owner of two additional Express offices in Albert Lea, Minnesota, and Cedar Falls, Iowa. The hope and support Express offers those seeking work is what Betsy loves most about her job. "My favorite part of being an Express franchisee is seeing a plan come together and helping people help themselves," she said. "At Express, we are enabling everyone to be profitable by providing career opportunities and staffing solutions."

Express has seen substantial growth during the last 30 years, and Betsy has been part of it all. She has enjoyed meeting new people and gaining lasting friendships, something she says has been the best part of her career with Express.

Due to the success Betsy created for herself and her franchise, she was able to take her children on that trip to Disney World. "It took me three years to get them there, but I did it!"

Today, Betsy enjoys spending time with her children and grandchildren. She also does a lot of volunteering within her community and is an active member of several organizations and community boards, including the Owatonna Foundation, Relay for Life, and Chamber of Commerce. Betsy is a past president of several community clubs and is on the Board of Directors for the Steele County Food Shelf. "I like doing that," Betsy said. "If I ever decide to retire, I would still volunteer."

Betsy looks forward to seeing Express continue to grow. "I love watching the younger generation come in and seeing the excitement they have to declare their own destiny and own their business," Betsy said. "It's a major success point for Express."

Roberta Long
Like Night and Day

Roberta Long's early years were filled with poverty and heartache. She never had new clothes, only hand-me-downs or used items provided through charities. Her dad left the family, and her mom struggled to raise Roberta along with her three sisters.

Growing up, Roberta had difficulty in school, failing many of her courses and eventually dropping out. "I had a hearing problem that wasn't diagnosed until I was older," Roberta said, "At the time I just thought I was stupid because that's what everyone was calling me. I didn't think I could do better."

Roberta turned to alcohol and drugs in an attempt to ease her pain. "My life was horrible. I married and had two children, but I could barely manage to take care of them. I was angry, abusive, and a terrible mother. It was a nightmare. Then I had two more children whom I decided to give up for adoption."

Roberta found herself at the lowest point in her life. "I wanted to end my life but I heard a voice inside me say, 'Where are you going?' I wondered if there was a God? I began to read the Bible and realized that when I died, I would be going somewhere, either heaven or hell, and it was a choice I needed to make. So I accepted Jesus and got saved. The most amazing thing was how God delivered me from all those drugs," Roberta said.

Right away, Roberta started building positive relationships with the couple who adopted her two youngest children. From their earliest years, the children got to know Roberta as their birth mother. She even reached out to both her ex-husband and her father.

Roberta also went back to school, graduating with a 3.7 grade point average from an adult high school in Dinuba, California.

"My graduating just proves those people were wrong when they said I was stupid," Roberta said.

Roberta's neighbor, Nathan Jefferson, works for Express Employment Professionals. He admired the way she was turning her life around. When he heard that Roberta and her children were about to lose their home, Nathan got her a job interview.

"Express got me in for an appointment really fast," Roberta said. "They got me work so that I could pay some of my bills. The people at Express went out of their way, even helping me with groceries and gas."

Unfortunately, Roberta and her family were evicted and were homeless for six months. During those months, Express kept calling Roberta back and finding her temporary jobs. Eventually, they got her a steady job at a bakery where she packs pretzels, tracks boxes, and takes care of paperwork.

"I love what I do at the bakery, and it's awesome that I can actually pay all my bills now," Roberta said. "My kids and I are together again in a nice apartment, and I just bought my first car. I'm not trying to have more than I need, but I'm just so thankful to the Lord and to Express that I now have enough to support my family. It's wonderful to take my kids out to eat and let them pick whatever they want off the menu. Mostly, I want to give them the opportunities I didn't have growing up. I want them to have paths to whatever careers they want."

Inder Narang
Determined to Succeed

Inder Narang was inspired by three men in his life: his late father, an uncle who became a successful entrepreneur, and his grandfather who built a career in the police force. Their examples pushed him to work hard and make something of himself.

Inder was born and raised in New Delhi, India. His family was able to pay for a university education for him and he graduated with a degree in mechanical engineering. Inder was determined to become totally independent and financially successful. He found a job right out of school, but after nine months, he discovered that there was no opportunity for advancement. As he researched other engineering positions that might be available, he became increasingly discouraged. There were very few openings. The work was hard and the pay was low.

Inder's brother had immigrated to the United States and he encouraged him to move as well. When Inder arrived in New York, he had great expectations but he soon found new obstacles to his dreams. The engineering positions he applied for required more experience than he had and he ended up working as a sales associate in a department store. Despite this setback, Inder constantly kept his eyes open for new opportunities and spent his free time researching engineering firms on the Internet.

After a year in New York, he decided that he should move to Los Angeles, California and look for work in the aerospace industry.

When Inder arrived in L.A., he had no job and no contacts. He managed to find a job as a machinist, but it was not what he ultimately wanted. Inder began working and going to a local community college to continue his studies in engineering. This was a difficult time because he didn't have a car and usually had to walk everywhere. Inder persevered, continuing to refine his skills, update his résumé, and apply to help wanted ads.

Fortunately for Inder, one of those ads was placed by Express Employment Professionals. After evaluating his skills and experience, the staff at Express immediately came up with two possible positions. The first job didn't work out because it was too far from where he lived and Inder didn't have transportation. However, when he interviewed at the second company they told him that he looked like the perfect match—someone willing to take on a variety of engineering assignments and ready to work hard to get ahead.

"After two and a half years of struggle in the U.S., I feel so lucky that I found Express," Inder said. "They took the time to find out what I wanted and then matched me with the perfect company. The work environment is great, my co-workers are nice, and I have the chance to move up if I do well."

Because of his job, Inder has been able to move into a new studio apartment and has extra spending money.

His goals in life are simple and straight-forward. He wants to earn the respect of his family and his co-workers. Although he is only 26, Inder seems well on his way to achieving all of his goals and then some.

"I am just grateful that I was able to move to America," he said. "There is so much more opportunity and a better lifestyle. I feel fortunate to be here."

People today don't often realize the difference their appearance makes. Cut-offs and T-shirts may seem to be the norm, but for Debi Nimz her professional dress made a great first impression that changed her life.

Debi worked in the banking industry in Kansas, Nebraska, and Oklahoma. In June 2004, the bank where she worked for eight years was sold to new owners. She was assured that her job would be safe, but as you can guess—on the day the new owners took over—130 people were laid off, and Debi was one of them.

"I had been working in the banking industry for 25 years, so I was devastated when I received a police escort out of the building that day," Debi said. "That was the worst day of my career. However, in another way, it was the best day of my career."

As part of her severance package, Debi was offered a résumé writing and interview seminar by Express Employment Professionals. "What was amazing to me was that out of the 130 people offered this opportunity, only six showed up," Debi said. "Also, one of the things that made me stand out was that I was the only one who dressed professionally to attend the seminar."

After the seminar, Cindy Fairchild, who managed the Oklahoma City Express office, approached Debi and told her she might have a job for her. She had Debi drive straight from the seminar to the Express office to apply for the position. That very day, Debi became an Express associate. After more interviews, Debi was hired at the Express International Headquarters on an evaluation hire basis. Within three months, she was hired full time and has been at headquarters ever since.

"Needless to say, I was willing to do whatever I needed to do to find a home with Express Employment Professionals," Debi said. "My happiness at work counted for a lot, and I knew that with hard work and dedication, everything would be fine. I just had my ninth anniversary with the company. I love Express and my job!

In helping someone else, I feel that is an accomplishment in itself...

Debi is now working in the Assistance Center at Express, providing support for the franchises on a daily basis. She travels the country helping new franchisees open their offices and making sure their business gets off to a good start.

"Every day, there are successes. In helping someone else, I feel that is an accomplishment in itself, and that's my job—to help other people," Debi said. "All because I dressed for success."

When Debi isn't helping Express offices, she enjoys spending time with her grandson.

Tina Padilla
A Perfect Fit

Anyone who likes to do jigsaw puzzles knows there's nothing more satisfying than finding that last puzzle piece and seeing it go in just right. For Tina Padilla, finding Express Employment Professionals was like that, a moment when everything finally fit into place.

"I spent lots of time on my grandparents' farm. I learned how to work, and I mean really work. I would feed the pigs and goats, and take care of the other animals. I learned to say yes sir and yes ma'am, and I listened to country music. Mostly, I learned to do an honest day's work for an honest day's pay," Tina said. "My parents emphasized the same values, especially my dad, who was a truck driver with a strong work ethic. He believed in loyalty to his company so much that he worked for one company until it closed and then stayed with his next employer for 30 years. He has been my inspiration all my life."

Tina's job history has been varied – and she likes it that way. Her hobby as a teenager was competing in roller skating competitions, so her very first job was working in the concession stand at the roller rink. Early in her career, Tina worked at a pipe manufacturing company, for a wholesale grocer, and in the trucking industry.

Tina quit work to be a stay-at-home mom until her children reached kindergarten age. Later in life, Tina went to college, earned her associate's degree, and found a position doing office work for a home appraiser.

In the years following, Tina worked for a bank as a courier delivering packets from the branch office to the bank's main office. She moved up to the supply area and was then promoted to mail room manager, where she supervised four other workers. When the bank was sold to new owners, however, the management moved its offices to Utah, so despite her hard work and dedication Tina, found herself out of a job.

Then, Tina found Express. She landed a job at a warehouse for a two-week temporary position that ended up lasting a year. When the assignment ended, she went back to Express and was assigned a position at another company in the mail room, where she worked her way up to office manager. In that position, she found herself contacting the Express office regularly to hire temporary workers the company needed.

"When the economy forced that company to close, I thought I was too old to try to go out and find a job, so I went on unemployment for a while, but I just couldn't live that way. It wasn't how I was raised. Before long, I went straight back to Express to find work."

Express found a job for Tina with a local mill. Her assignment was for a couple of months and she was there almost a year. The next assignments were the same, and while working one assignment, Tina received a request from another job asking her to come back temporarily. Tina knows if she wants to work, Express will find a job for her.

Tina now says she is officially retired, but whenever she decides she wants a part-time job she goes to Express to see what's available.

"With Express, I know I can depend on them to find me a job that actually fits me and my situation," Tina said. "All I can say is that when someone needs a job I tell them to try Express because I've found, even in rough times, Express will get you working."

Joe Paquette
A Purpose Along with a Career

During his first summer job in college, Joe Paquette built swimming pools, a strenuous job that involved heavy lifting and manual labor under the scorching Oklahoma sun. At the end of that summer, Joe vowed to avoid construction as his life's work. When he returned to college in the fall, Joe declared business as his major and it was a true turning point in his life.

In an interesting parallel, Express Employment Professionals was growing and maturing during those same years. Joe had a friend who interned at an Express office, and he knew several other people who found temporary jobs through the staffing company. In addition, Express had an office less than a mile away from the house Joe had grown up in, so he passed it almost every day. However, it was at Oklahoma Baptist University during the fall semester that Joe began to connect with people from Express.

In 2000, Joe took a course called Intro to Business. His professor, David Gillogly, had retired from serving as president of Express, but still served as company director. David became Joe's favorite teacher and mentor.

Coincidentally, the next summer, Joe worked at the Express Angus Ranch in Shawnee, feeding cattle and taking care of livestock. The ranch's owner is Bob Funk, who is also the CEO of Express. With connections like these, it is no wonder that Joe was hired right after college graduation for a temporary job in the accounting department at Express International Headquarters.

A few months later, Joe moved to an Express office in Oklahoma City to work as a staffing consultant, helping connect people with the right jobs. From there, Joe was assigned to a team of young professionals opening a new office in downtown Oklahoma City.

Early in his career with Express, Joe had an encounter with Bob Funk that he says will always stick in his mind. Joe and several of his co-workers were celebrating a milestone. They decided to spend some of their bonus checks on a fancy breakfast at a nearby restaurant. To everyone's surprise, there across the way sat Bob Funk. "Since I remembered him from the year I worked at the ranch, I urged my buddies to all go chat with him and tell him about hitting our big goal, so they did," Joe said. "Then Bob asked what we'd want if we managed to reach an even bigger sales goal. Usually, I'm sort of shy, but something came over me, and I said I'd want a cowboy hat like his.

"He laughed and wrote it down but none of us thought much about the conversation. A few months later, the office achieved its goal. And I'll be darned if there was a hat just like Bob's sitting on my desk the next day," he said. "That was pretty neat."

Joe has been with Express for more than five years and is now back at headquarters, working with several of the people he actually helped hire years ago.

"I've worn lots of different hats in my years here at Express," Joe said. "And through it all, I have loved my job. We're always helping people. I get to see lives changed. I have a purpose along with a career."

And, Joe still cherishes that cowboy hat Bob Funk gave him.

Finding a job in a small town can be difficult. Finding a job with enough flexibility to attend college classes and still leave one with time to study, can be even more challenging.

But when Megan Plopper's friends suggested that Express Employment Professionals could help her find a job to accommodate her class schedule, Megan immediately scheduled an appointment.

Megan was impressed with the honesty of her staffing consultant when he explained from the beginning that the only jobs he could offer her would be temporary assignments due to her schedule. Megan enjoyed the variety of jobs because she learned different skill sets. She worked with Express for two months and then accepted an internship with the State of Illinois. Following her internship, as she neared graduation at Benedictine University at Springfield, Illinois, the psychology major again turned to Express.

"I really had no clue how hard it was going to be to find a job," she said. "After two months of sending out résumés and filling out applications, I asked Express for help. They quickly found me a job as a case worker helping low income families find assistance."

Unfortunately Megan's job was eliminated by budget cuts, and she returned to Express seeking another position. She was pleasantly surprised when they offered her a job working in their office. She accepted on the spot and went to work as a receptionist.

Shortly thereafter, the love of her life convinced her to relocate with him from Illinois to Kansas.

Megan hoped moving to another state might yield a job that would make use of her degree. Once in Kansas, Megan began her job search again and took several volunteer positions within the community. She still had expenses from college to repay so she called Express once more.

"I wasn't worried because I knew from past experience that if you want to work, Express will help you find something," Megan said. "It doesn't matter what level of education you have, they will help you find a job. Their level of professionalism is the best. After a couple of months in a job, they'll follow up with you. If you aren't happy with what you are doing, they'll find you something else. They want people to be happy in their jobs."

Megan says her life has changed as the result of her relationship with Express Employment Professionals. Express once gave her a book called, *First Thing Every Morning*. It's a book that she still reads daily for inspiration.

"I learned different skills at each job to make me well-rounded," Megan said. "So now when I go to apply for a job, I feel I am more likely to be picked because I have experience in so many areas."

Megan's goal is to find a job working with youth, instilling in them a positive outlook on life. She knows that Express Employment Professionals will be there to help her reach that goal.

Sherry Preston
Persistence Pays

After she graduated from high school in Bartlesville, Oklahoma, Sherry Preston was anxious to leave town and start a new life. She wanted to move to California to live with her dad. Before she left, Sherry met her soon-to-be husband, Mike, who went with her to California where they were married.

During her time in California, Sherry endured many trying times which would test her strength and courage. In 2001, Mike passed away leaving Sherry a widow and a single mom at a relatively young age. Despite her tragedy, she forged ahead and went to work for the district attorney's office in Ventura County. "I really liked the work because I was making an impact in people's lives," Sherry said.

Unfortunately, that job didn't last very long. The position was eliminated due to state budget cuts. It was the start of a long and difficult time in California's economy and there weren't many job opportunities.

Sherry decided it was a good time to move back to Bartlesville where the economy was stronger and she could be near her sister, as well as her extended family.

Once in Oklahoma, Sherry landed a job at a local insurance agency but the position didn't offer any opportunity for advancement and she was laid off after three years. Not to be deterred, she tenaciously pursued a new job and submitted her application to all three staffing companies in town. "I called the three employment agencies every day, every morning at eight o'clock."

Her persistence paid off. One morning, she made her daily phone call to Express Employment Professionals. They had an opening and asked how soon she could be on the job. An hour and a half later, she was on a temporary assignment that lasted two weeks. During that time, Sherry proved she was willing to go above and beyond in her job. The two-week assignment turned into nine months. That job led to another nine-month temporary position. The company was so impressed with Sherry they hired her full time. "If it wasn't for Express, I would never have gotten my foot in the door and been able to secure a full-time position with this company," Sherry said.

She now lives a very satisfying life. Sherry has her own apartment, a good car, and can afford to pursue hobbies she once could not. She dabbles in photography, jewelry making, and crocheting.

"It's been wonderful. This job has made a big difference in my life," Sherry said. "I can do some of the extras that I was not able to before. Life is so much better."

It's been wonderful. This job has made a big difference in my life...I can do some of the extras that I was not able to do before. Life is so much better.

Renee Rodriquez
From Temp to the Top

A six-month internship, and a chance meeting with a local business owner, would lead to a lifetime of fulfillment for Renee Rodriquez.

Renee attended college at the University of Southern Colorado in Pueblo and had just completed a six-month internship with the Pueblo Chamber of Commerce when she met Dionne Casey, the owner of the local Express Employment Professionals office. When Renee completed her six-month internship she decided to go straight to Express for a temporary job until she found permanent employment. Bill Casey, Dionne's husband, interviewed Renee and had her complete a computer evaluation. "I had a message on my answering machine when I got home that Express had found an assignment for me. I thought that was pretty cool," she said.

Renee's temporary job with a manufacturing company lasted a couple of weeks. While she was on a one week assignment at an airplane brake company, Bill asked if Renee would like to work for them in their Express office. "I still was working part time at the chamber office and also at a TV station, so I had to give my two weeks' notice. For a few weeks, I had several jobs. It was pretty hectic, but I could not believe my luck," she said.

Right after Renee started working with the Caseys in their Express office, they became really busy. After five years of working together, the Caseys asked if Renee would like to become a partner. "I was raising my two sons as a single mom, so I didn't see how that could be financially possible, but then they explained that my payments for the partnership would come out of my profit sharing checks. Obviously, I said yes! What a blessing the Caseys have been in my life! I don't know what

they saw in me or why, but I owe everything to them."

About five years later, the Caseys decided they were ready to retire and wanted to sell their franchise. The new buyer wanted 100 percent of the company, but the Casey's worked out a deal where Renee could continue to work for the new owner.

A few years later, when the new owner decided to move, Renee became majority partner of the Pueblo office with Eric Carson. Renee had met Eric eight years prior when she was awarded the Business Woman of the Year by the United States Hispanic Chamber of Commerce. Eric believed in Renee and joined her as her partner in life and business.

"The people at Express have been so wonderful to me during these 25 years," she said. "I've worked hard, and people have given me opportunities I never thought I'd have. I have three children who've all been involved in the business." Renee's older son, Derrick, and his wife, Diana, work with Renee, along with her youngest daughter, Taylor. Renee's son, Kevin, has helped them on many occasions, making her business a family affair. "What a great thing that is to be able to do for your children. It has been wonderful to be able to help them with their dreams and to give them something to look forward to down the road," Renee said.

Most of all, Renee loves the fact that she can have a career where she can help change people's lives. "And here I am, a perfect example of that very concept," she said. "I walked in here just to find a temporary job until I found something permanent, and look what happened."

Renee and Eric now own both the Pueblo and Centennial, Colorado offices.

Helen Simmons
A Lifeline Just in Time

Helen Simmons began working for Express Employment Professionals in 2010 after the economic downturn forced her to close the custom painting business she and her daughter had been running in Skagit County, Washington.

"No one was spending any money but I kept hoping things would turn around," Helen said. Sadly, she eventually lost her home as well as her business. Desperate for work, Helen remembers calling Express when she realized she had to do something just to cover her basic living expenses.

'They called me back right away and within a few days they found me a job," she said. "I went to work for Express and I haven't looked back. I rarely turn down an assignment unless it is physically too difficult. I have trouble with my knee now so I can't stand for hours, but I am ready for most jobs. Of course, I am hoping to find that one dream job, but in the meantime I like the challenge of taking on different positions."

Helen enjoys staying busy and working in the variety of jobs that Express offers her. One of her first assignments was counting boxes of frozen fish on a dock. "That job might have been a test to see how willing I was to work," she said.

Some of the other positions Helen recalls include working at a local firehouse as a receptionist and administrative assistant, organizing a dinner and auction which raised $150,000 for a local nonprofit organization, and working for an interior design firm. An exceptional Express associate, Helen's talents, flexibility and strong work ethic were rewarded when Express selected her as the Administrative Employee of the Year in 2012.

Helen appreciates all the support she has received from the Mount Vernon, Washington office. "Everyone there is very nice and very professional. They make a point of knowing who you are and letting you know they care about you."

Helen has also made new friends working at different companies, which has been an unexpected bonus. "I am a relationship person and so one of the things I enjoy most is getting to meet new people," she said. "Working for Express gives me that opportunity. Express threw me a lifeline when I truly needed one."

I am hoping to find that one dream job,
but in the meantime
I like the challenge of taking on different positions.

With his unemployment running out and money from his retirement package dwindling, Frank Robert Smith was really hurting financially. The former drug store assistant manager had lost his job and spent many nights sleeping in his car.

"I had hit rock bottom and was more than ready to make a fresh start at something worthwhile," Frank said.

"I was almost out of hope when I went to the public library and used the computer to Google temp agencies in Northeast Massachusetts. The one that sounded most appealing was Express," Frank said.

I had hit rock bottom and was more than ready to make a fresh start at something worthwhile.

From his very first interview, Frank really felt confident that the people at Express could help him. "When I went to meet them, they made a positive impression on me," he said. "They showed me respect and seemed to want to get to know me as an individual to find out what kind of work would suit me."

When they saw how much Frank wanted to work, Express found him quite a few job assignments. Because he wasn't afraid to stock shelves, unload trucks, sweep floors, and rake lawns, Frank showed how determined a worker he could be. "At first it troubled me a lot that I was doing menial labor when I have my bachelor's degree," Frank said, "but the people at Express taught me to appreciate the jobs I got and to make the best of each one. Now, when I get jobs that involve a bit more responsibility, I really appreciate them.

"I thought Express was pretty terrific in what they did for me. The jobs have done wonders for my self-confidence," he said.

One job in particular that has boosted Frank's confidence is a warehouse delivery position. That experience brought back much of the truck driving skills Frank acquired during college to help pay for his expenses. He is now considering truck driving as a career.

"Things are looking up now," he said. "I think by driving a truck, I'll make enough money and have enough time to try my hand at my newest hobby: writing. Right now, I'm writing blog articles that describe products for sale on the Internet. For example, if someone wants to sell motorcycle boots, I'll write the ad to help that person get more sales. Of course, my goal is to write a book eventually and I think I can do it."

Christy Taylor was raised to know right from wrong. Her parents, the Skojecs, taught her early in life to do the right thing. She credits her father for her Type A personality, her drive, and her competitive spirit. She acquired her nurturing disposition and concern for those less fortunate from her mom. Together, Christy's parents challenged her to set high goals and, hopefully, find ways to help others.

Born in New York, Christy grew up moving from town to town all along the Eastern Seaboard before settling in Rocky Mount, North Carolina, where she graduated from Wesleyan University with a bachelor's degree in history. She planned to become a historian at one of the state parks, but desired a career that offered financial stability with the chance to help others.

Then came her golden opportunity when Christy took a position with the Rocky Mount Express Employment Professionals office. She was barely on the job two weeks when, suddenly, every person in the office quit. For six months Christy was the only worker at the Express office. "I have always been an ethical person," Christy said. "In my opinion those people acted very unethical when they left. I didn't miss them at all, so I managed just fine."

And manage she did. For 20 years, Christy remained at that same office, eventually buying into the franchise. She and her mother now own the business together with another partner. "We have nine employees, so we have grown a lot. We even went through a horrible flood back in 1999, but we recovered right away and haven't looked back since," she said.

The philosophy at Express matched Christy in every way. "I really don't think I could have found another business that mirrors how my parents raised me so well," she said. "Express has given me the opportunity to make a good living while also helping take care of people, something that is near and dear to me."

Christy enjoys reminiscing about the people she has worked with through the years and one of her biggest success stories is Aubrey, whom she put to work at a local oil change place 20 years ago. "When I hired Aubrey, he was really down on his luck and he didn't have a car. Another employee told me he'd seen Aubrey walking to work in the rain on several occasions and stopped to give him a ride. I knew with that determination he would eventually be hired full time with the company. He is still there today. When I go to have my oil changed, Aubrey is always the first one to smile and say hello. It makes me happy to know he has had a better life and a steady income for all these years because we believed in him."

Christy's career with Express has also afforded her opportunities to give back to her community, helping numerous people along the way. She is currently on the board of the local United Way and volunteers as a guardian ad litem for the foster care system, serving as an advocate for foster children by making sure the courts and social service agencies are making decisions that are in the best interest of the children. Christy also spends time fostering dogs and helping transport them to loving homes.

Because of Express, Christy has had a successful career and fulfilling life.

Eric Urban
A Second Chance at Life

Eric Urban is determined to become a national park ranger–a goal he set his sights on when working at Yellowstone National Park. Majoring in fish and wildlife management at Montana State University, Eric was about to finish his degree and move one step closer to achieving his goal.

However, tragedy struck when his parents had passed away. "That news just threw me off the tracks," Eric said. "I could not understand how that could possibly have happened. Even now, I have lots of questions, but one thing was for sure, my life went on a downward slide from there."

Eric dropped out of college so he could travel repeatedly from Montana to Ohio to deal with the details of his parents' estates. Eric spent almost two years fighting with banks, credit card companies, and insurance companies, but he ended up with next to nothing.

In desperation, Eric was at a jewelry store in downtown Bozeman trying to sell his mother's jewelry just to make ends meet. That's when he realized he really needed to get back into the workforce.

But he didn't know what to do. His parent's tragic passing scarred him psychologically. He suffered from social anxiety and felt terrified about being in public. His counselor advised him to try temporary work at first.

"I just wanted to dip my toes into the labor pool because I knew I was still too nervous to go for a full-time job," Eric said. "After leaving the jewelry store, I was walking aimlessly down the streets of Bozeman when I happened to pass by the Express Employment Professionals office. I remember thinking to myself. I ought to give this a try. I told the owners Rina and Greg Donaldson my whole story, and they were immediately very supportive of me."

The staff at Express managed to ease Eric back into the workforce. They started by offering him only stress-free assignments. If Eric felt at all uncomfortable about a particular job or didn't like an assignment, he would let Express know right away so they could find him another job. Slowly, by working at various short-term assignments, Eric regained his confidence.

"It was just what I needed," Eric said. "Not only was the monetary compensation good, but I also began to feel a little bit better each time I successfully completed an assignment. Recently, I've been working in the tourism industry where I'm once again greeting the public. Every day, I gain more confidence."

Eric's future looks much brighter now.

I'm proud to say I think I'm finally ready to go out and get what I want.

"I finally got tired of pitying myself and realized what a gift life is," Eric said. "Despite everything that happened, my parents gave me my life and they gave me opportunities to make something of myself. I'm proud to say I think I'm finally ready to go out and get what I want."

Eric plans to enroll again at Montana State University and eventually complete his degree to become a park ranger. The road ahead may be steep, but he thinks he'll make it and so does the team at Express.

Deidra Viney
From Lemonade Stands to Express Employment Professionals

Deidra Viney was born a salesperson. Growing up in Philadelphia, she loved setting up lemonade stands and selling Girl Scout cookies. In high school, she joined Future Business Leaders of America and held her first steady job as a babysitter for her neighbor's kids. When Deidra headed off to college, she majored in finance and interned with a bank. After graduation, the bank offered her a full-time job as a commercial lender, helping fledgling companies get business loans.

Deidra always wanted to own a business and, as she interviewed entrepreneurs during the loan process, she was fascinated with their business ventures. In her spare time, she began researching possible business opportunities. When she looked at franchises, she saw the advantage of having a support system.

"I knew I wanted a business that would not take up all of my time 365 days of the year," she said. "It needed to be something that would fit my personality and yet be an endeavor that would stay around for years, not something seasonal or fly-by-night. I considered cleaning companies and vending companies, and even went to franchise expos to see if anything appealed to me, but nothing seemed to be the right fit."

Eventually, Deidra honed-in on staffing companies because they met so many of her criteria. "I was looking at various staffing providers. They were courting me, and I was courting them," she said. "Then one day I happened to strike up a conversation with an acquaintance who was a business broker, so I asked him if he knew of any franchises for sale and he recommended Express."

After that day, Deidra put Express Employment Professionals on her list. The more she found out about them, the more she liked them. "From the very beginning, their professionalism won me over, and the rest—as they say—is history. That was 13 years ago," she said.

Deidra's office is located in Jersey City, New Jersey, and as she gazes out her office window across the Hudson River to the New York City skyline, she often thinks about how much she loves her business. "I think it's exciting to see people find work so they can provide for their families," Deidra said. "I also love the other end of the staffing process, helping businesses fill their needs with the right people. It makes me feel good to be able to provide them with good employees."

Deidra always stresses to job seekers how much of a difference a positive outlook can make on any person's career. "One time, a client called saying he needed someone in his office for only two days. We tried offering this opportunity to several people, but they kept turning us down. Finally, we found one lady who agreed to go to work for those two days. The company loved her and hired her full time. She eventually became their office manager, so now she calls us all the time for workers."

Deidra definitely practices what she preaches. Her positive attitude has always led to her success—whether it was selling cookies or now running a top staffing business.

Lorenzo Thomas Wallace
Just Keep Going Forward

To most people, having to endure a lifetime of struggles just to survive would seem like a terrible injustice. Never knowing if there will be enough money to make it to the next month would be emotionally exhausting. To most, it would be easy to give up. Lorenzo Thomas Wallace is not most people. Never complaining, never giving up, Lorenzo learned from a very young age to "just keep going forward."

He was born in Spotsylvania County, Virginia, and grew up in a humble, two-bedroom house with his parents and two brothers. Lorenzo's mother was a housewife and his father was a logger in the vast woodlands that comprise much of Spotsylvania County. They worked hard to provide for their three growing boys, but times were tough. With no running water, the family pumped water from a well and took baths in an outside tub with water warmed by the sun.

School was a battle for Lorenzo. After struggling to master the basics, he quit in the ninth grade and set out on his own to begin what would become a constant struggle to find work.

There was one bright spot among Lorenzo's daily struggles. In the early 90s, he fell in love with a girl named Kathy. Originally from Pittsburgh, Kathy and her daughter moved to Virginia after her first husband died. She and her friends would go out on Friday nights. It was then that Kathy and Lorenzo first met.

Lorenzo liked to dance. His two-step won Kathy's heart and they've been enduring life's ups and downs together ever since. "Everyone always teases us, they don't know how a country boy and a city girl ever got together," Kathy said.

Living paycheck to paycheck was not unusual for Lorenzo and Kathy, but in 2009 they hit rock bottom when he lost his job and they lost their home. After searching for jobs for a year and a half, Lorenzo found Express Employment Professionals.

Express was instrumental in finding Lorenzo work. Although none of the jobs have had much longevity, they have paid well. Express has kept him consistently employed with various companies in the Richmond area. He also finds side jobs in the neighborhood cutting grass, hauling brush, and scrapping metal.

"I do what I can to survive," Lorenzo said.

"He takes care of our family," Kathy said. "He's one of a kind."

Perseverance, generosity, humility, and love of family define him. By every measure of a man, Lorenzo sets the standard high.

This positive attitude has carried him through a trying life. "The only thing I'm gonna do is just keep going forward," Lorenzo said.

Felicia Walls
A World Turned Upside Down

Felicia Walls spent six years in the Army Reserve and loved every single minute of it. Afterwards, the Washington native spent 14 years in customer service, a field in which she thrived. Felicia enjoyed working and her future looked very promising.

"Then it happened," Felicia said. "My life was turned upside down."

Felicia left her office one day during the lunch hour to drive to a nearby eatery for a bite when she was rear-ended while waiting at a traffic light. "I had a shoulder injury that damaged the tendons and ligaments and required surgery, which just doesn't heal very fast. About a year later, I was almost back to feeling good when I was hit a second time, this time by a drunk driver. I couldn't even sit down without hurting, and I certainly couldn't go back to work."

Then it happened...
My life was turned
upside down.

After another couple of years of rehabilitation, Felicia finally healed enough from the accidents and started thinking about finding a new job. "I just wanted to test the waters," Felicia said. "I didn't feel like I could approach employers and say I could work for them if I actually couldn't. I wanted to ease back into the workforce with some type of part-time or temporary position and that is when I became associated with the folks at Express Employment Professionals. They were so enthusiastic and helpful. They have been wonderful at finding me the perfect jobs where I have been able to work without being in too much pain. In fact, I have been able to handle every job I've been sent on."

The types of jobs Felicia has accepted have been varied, but that's fine with her. She's worked at a car dealership, answered phones, and became proficient at data entry.

"I really like the idea that my jobs have been so different and challenging in their own ways," she said.

"Today, I don't stress about work like I used to," Felicia said. "My shoulder has finally healed enough, so I'm beginning to look for a full-time job, something with benefits, hopefully."

Now that Felicia is starting to feel stronger, she enjoys spending time with her two rat terriers. "I like to ride my bike in the beautiful parks around here. I don't go very fast, so my dogs manage to stay up with me. We also love to go what I call dog-park hopping. I take them from one scenic dog park to another. In between, the terriers hop in my car and take naps till we get to the next stop. Then they jump out ready to play again. They are a lot of fun."

With the support of the staff at Express, her friends, and her two dogs, Felicia has kept a positive attitude toward her job hunt, confident that her next assignment just might be a full-time position.

Murray Glenn Whitaker
Following a Calling

When Murray Glenn Whitaker left home in Thornton, Colorado, a suburb of Denver, to pursue a singing and songwriting career in Los Angeles, he had stars in his eyes. He also had some influential connections with producers already in show business, so Murray and his band enjoyed several significant performances, including a few cameo appearances for television.

It wasn't long after Murray moved to California that he had a change of heart. "After hearing a message from the World Mission Society Church of God, I had a revelation," Murray said. "I realized the celebrity lifestyle wasn't for me."

Murray left California behind and returned home to Colorado, where he became deeply involved with the Church of God.

Before long, Murray was named a deacon and began leading Bible studies. The Denver branch of his church soon asked him to move to Pueblo, two and a half hours south of Denver to participate in the gospel work of evangelizing the southern Colorado area. He gladly accepted the calling.

When Murray got to Pueblo, he wanted to help the church in any way possible but he also wanted to work full time. He went online and learned about Express Employment Professionals.

After completing an online registration, Murray went to the Express office. "Right away, the Express staff worked with me to find a job that I truly enjoyed with the hope of permanent placement at a position that could eventually help shape my career. I've been working as an office administrator and doing accounts receivable and I love it!"

Now Murray lives to share his faith and spread the good news about his Express family as well.

Right away, the Express staff worked with me to find a job...

Izeal Wilson
A Better Spot

It's often trying for children to appreciate the wisdom of their parents. For Izeal Wilson, the regret of not trusting his parent's wisdom when he was young still gnaws at him. Now older and having his own children, Izeal is working hard to overcome the mistakes he says he made early in life.

Izeal's parents didn't intend for him to have such a unique name. They had chosen Isaiah, a Biblical name. However, somewhere between his parent's intentions and a midwife who was responsible for recording his information, the name Isaiah became Izeal. Izeal was born in Stamford, Connecticut, a coastal community on Long Island Sound. His dad was an electrician by trade and worked hard to provide for his family. But his parents could never afford to buy a house of their own, so Izeal grew up in low-income housing which provided a shelter but not a home.

"We managed," Izeal said. "I did all the things other kids did. Although I didn't try out for school sports, I loved to play basketball in the neighborhood."

Like many young people, Izeal didn't always listen to the advice of the adults in his life. "I didn't really listen to my elders as I should have. Now that I'm older I realize, if I had, maybe I would be in a better spot," he said.

Izeal had his first child when he was in high school so he had to start working at an early age. He dropped out of school and began doing cabinetry, woodwork, and various other jobs. Realizing the importance of an education, he eventually went back to school to earn his GED but still struggled to find permanent work.

Eager to find better employment, Izeal contacted Express. "I asked for the address and I shot on down there," he said.

The first two jobs Express found for Izeal were temporary jobs. The third position ended up being permanent. Because of Izeal's outstanding work ethic, he recently received Employee of the Year honors. "The award was an extra motivator. I was nominated and I won. It made me feel really good," Izeal said.

Now, Izeal is focused on the future. His short-term goal is to go back to school and get his commercial driver's license. He hopes to be able to drive a truck and provide more for his family. His family is what keeps him motivated. He also knows the importance of being a good father and credits own dad for shaping his character. "I have four children and I want to work hard and set an example for them," he said.

Izeal's father passed away recently and the sting from the loss is still fresh. Someday Izeal might be able to let go of the regret of his childhood. For now, it still lingers. But his hard work and determination are sure to put him "in a better spot."

Christopher Yaniz
No Easy Path

A teacher's influence can have a profound impact on a student's life. Such was the case with Mrs. Sanchez and Christopher Yaniz. At first, he thought his middle school teacher was always sticking her nose into his affairs.

"She didn't like the people I was hanging around with and repeatedly called my adoptive mom to let her know. She sat me down one day and talked to me about how I needed to make friends with people who had more of the same interests. She told me if I stayed with people who were too laid back to work and who caused trouble at school, my future would not look good," Christopher said. "Today, I realize how much Mrs. Sanchez helped me turn a corner in my life. It goes to show that school teachers can make a big difference in a young person's future, so now I volunteer with several nonprofit organizations to help children who've had similar experiences."

I think about all my experiences and I just say to myself, 'Hey, I'm a fighter.'

He went on to graduate from vocational school with skills as a graphic designer, but that field wasn't as interesting to him as he thought it would be. "So there I was searching for a job in the middle of the recession. I was struggling to find work. I was young and inexperienced. It was a hard time for me. Then I met Vicki Perez and her team at Express Employment Professionals. They helped me get through the tough times," he said.

Christopher's path took quite a few twists during those years as Express sent him all over Miami, Florida placing him in different industries with each new assignment. "I loved it because I learned so much," Christopher said. "I had all sorts of jobs. I worked in property management, insurance, the health field, and automotive industry. I even worked on the beach selling candy. No matter what the job was, I was able to expand my résumé and gain experience."

A positive attitude and willingness to learn helped Christopher stand out as an employee, and soon he was making the right connections with the right people. During a short stint at a bank, Christopher found himself assisting the human resources director. "She was impressed by how hard I worked," Christopher said, "Later when she moved to a new position she called me about a full-time opening there. I've only been on the job a short while, but I can already tell I am going to enjoy it."

Christopher plans to keep on climbing. "I think about all my experiences and I just say to myself, 'Hey, I'm a fighter.' No matter what obstacles are in front of me, I've gone through much, much worse. Now, I want a career. I have goals and I appreciate all the people, including the team at Express, who are helping me progress toward those goals."

Dawn Yengich
The Right Place at the Right Time

Dawn Yengich worked hard all her life. But the single mother learned one of the hardest lessons of all after college: even with education and a great work ethic, it sometimes takes contacts to find the perfect job.

Dawn was born and raised in Pueblo, Colorado. All-American in its history and values, Pueblo is known as the "Home of Heroes" and Dawn grew up with her own personal hero close at hand and in her heart–her grandmother. "My grandma did it all: maintaining a career, keeping a spotless house, and putting dinner on the table every day," Dawn said. Watching her juggle everything taught Dawn about work ethic.

Bright and independent, Dawn moved to Denver her senior year of high school. Although she only lacked three credit hours, the district required her to attend school for an entire year in order to graduate. Determined that nothing would slow her down, Dawn got a job at a federal agency and juggled both school and work.

After high school, she returned home to help her mother and found herself maintaining a home, caring for a family, working full time, and going to college.

While taking care of her son, Dawn earned an associate's degree and set her eyes on the next goal–her bachelor's. Doing it all wasn't easy, but Dawn believed that "you do what you have to do." She took on a full-time job at the State of Colorado Revenue Department, attended college full time, and maintained a good home for her child. Unfortunately some college courses interfered with her work schedule, so Dawn transferred schools and drove almost 50 miles each way to complete her degree.

By the time she finished college, Dawn married and had two children. Even with a job and her family to care for, Dawn went on to earn a master's degree. When she and her husband later divorced, Dawn felt her responsibilities even more deeply. "I needed to make sure my family was taken care of," she said. Dawn took on a series of jobs, each one adding to her experience but none leading to the career path she desired.

Contracts ended and layoffs came along, and even though she had a history of rebounding quickly, Dawn finally hit a wall. "I was on unemployment for 14 or 15 months," she said. "So many times I heard I was overqualified. I interviewed for every job that I could. I went on so many interviews, it hurt my confidence."

For the first time in her life, Dawn found herself without a job and without any prospects. Then, she visited the Express Employment Professionals website and read through the job opportunities. Dawn interviewed for a job with Express on a Friday and was working by Monday. The position was a two-month trial. Through that job came an offer for another position. With encouragement from Express, Dawn took the job and remains there today.

Dawn recently took a trip to Europe, where her daughter performed with a folk dancing group. Being able to afford such opportunities reflects the security of Dawn's new life, settled in a permanent job.

Dawn credits Express with getting her into the right place at the right time. "I looked so hard for a job, and even with my education, I couldn't find one," she said. "Express helped me, and things have been great ever since."